In Between The Lines

In Between The Lines

BRINDA ROY

Anecdote
Publishing House
For the love of quality reading!

Anecdote
Publishing House
For the love of quality reading!

Anecdote Publishing House
2nd Floor 2/15 Lane no. 2 Ansari Road, Daryaganj-110002
Email: info@anecdotepublishinghouse.com
Website: anecdotepublishinghouse.com

Published by Anecdote Publishing House

First Edition 2025
ISBN 978-81-982589-3-9
MRP ₹ 299

Book Promoted and Marketed by Champ Readers Pvt. Ltd.
Cover design by The Book Bakers
Layout by Graphic Tailor
Printed by Thomson Press (India) Ltd, New Delhi

Contents

ALONE BUT NOT LONELY

POEM NO. 1

Once More...

Sweet musical enchanting words
Words that brought a spark in my heart
Words that could melt my heart of rock
Words that brought tears in those eyes
"Oh! Will he love me the way he says he will"?
I wondered day and night
The dreams he is feeding me
Are they for real to see....
My soul he wants to touch
Should I show him how bruised?
It already is
Will he really keep it with care?
If I give him my all
So let's give it a chance
And plunge again in the sea of love
He will not let me drown this time
He will help me grow and love me
That's all I ever wished for
Someone's true love
Love that is enigmatic

Love that is untamed
Love that knows no bound
Unrestrained
Meaninglessly meaningful
Crazily peaceful
Nothing else nothing at all
A love not deceitful…

ANIMAL INSTINCT

POEM NO. 2

Remembering You...

Sipping my chai after my morning walk
I sit near that road side stall
Where you first took me…
A small nook around the corner
Our nook I used to say
For a month we went there everyday
I used to sip my tea
And you used to look at me
Simply stare
And make me feel nervous
So nervous that the clumsy me
Often felt shy
But now…
I sit here alone
Alone with those memories
You left me with
Alone with those evocations
You left me with
You brought a smile
On my not so smiling face

And so easily
You could erase it all away
My beaming eyes weren't attractive enough
To keep you yearning for my presence
My anxious extension
Made you run away…
That's ok…
You would never understand a person like me
Who loves even when not loved back
Who prays even when you ghost attack
May your thirsty soul find peace elsewhere
In silence I will sip my chai
My small nook, me….
Reminiscence and
The passer byes….

BAITING IT THROUGH

POEM NO. 3

The Screen And Me...

When I keep on texting you
And you don't reply back
I keep staring at the screen
The way you used to look at me
Years back....
I keep staring for your one reply
Remember the day in college
The day you proposed
Your smile
Dimples behind your unkempt beard
Will you be mine forever
Yesss I said aloud
Yesss you heard
Yes, you hugged me tight
Yes, you did
Now that fifteen summers went by quick
Now that my lustrous hair not so thick
You look at me with indifferent distant

Love
You look at me with a disgust sigh…
The ring you gave me when you promised me a life
Where time will never replace deadlines….

BEING DAMAGED

POEM NO. 4

Yours Forever...

I can't be yours in this life
I am already taken
You can't love me.
A flower said
The grass whispered
I don't ask anything from you
You remain to whom you belong
But can't stop loving you my dear flower
As they spoke
A heavy thunder storm blew
Throughout that lighting night
The heavy rains mewed and barked
In the morning the first light
The grass saw the fragile sight
Lifeless with broken foliage
Sleeping peacefully under the
Bushes of sage
His dear flower
So gracefully calm
She will remain His
In all her forms...

Dream seller

POEM NO. 5

Yellow Daffodils...

The yellow Daffodils
That you presented me
Are still blooming on the hills
As I shower them with
My warmth and intimacy
With hope
That you will come back to
Me one fine day and say
Hey Lilly I am back
After winning the combat
With mankind unkind
Who claim to be protectors
But are monsters in disguise

I visit the hills everyday
My Daffodils sing to me
They dance and play
They try to bring a light
Of delight on my face
But where are you

I fail to find your trace…
Did they kill you?
Did they rip you apart?
For the heinous deed
They did
You protested took the lead

I know your bravery
Was something
You were known for
Something I admired in you
My love, I have your
Daffodils
You keep your fight
The uproar on
I will wait for you
An eternal wait
Through the dusk and the dawn

EKANTIKA

POEM NO. 6

Are You Real...

You touched my lips
With your tear filled eyes
How pure can love be
I wondered ....
That even when I fight
With you....
You hug me tight...
Your fingers which run through
My careless hair
Your words of appreciation
Makes me cherish
Your presence ....
I hated me so much
Before I met you
You made me
Fall in love with myself
With my body and soul
When you love me
Every moment of the day
I feel I rise from ashes

Like a phoenix
Your love is your encouragement
Your way of packing lunch
For me
Makes me feel so special
Such love, such pure passion
Is rare
Very rare…
Your selfless existence, your care
For being there
Makes me fall in love
With love again
Are you true
Or just my imagination….

WILD LOVE

POEM NO. 7

Self Love...

You highly believe in self-love
Congratulations to you
You always said
"I want to fulfill all my dreams
I want to dive into oceans
I want to dance with the brooks
I want to gallop with the horses"
And I used to listen to you
Look at your enthusiastic features
And wait, wait to hear
That you want me to be a part
A part of your dreams too….
Because my dreams were
Always on every side you stayed
For me self-love was loving you
For me hiding my pains
And dancing in your joy
Was loving myself
I waited simply waited
For that one call

That never came
But the wait was my way of loving you
And love my self
Self-love was all you cared for
Self-love was loving you

FLOWERS FOR THE SOUL

POEM NO. 8

Right To Love...

Innumerable texts
Countless calls
Those infinite sleepless nights
When you disregarded my prevalence
I believed you were over-embellished
I believe you were absorbed
With duties you call work
And I kept myself occupied
With your thoughts
Smelling your used shirts
Drinking your left over water
From the glass…
That touched your lips
I lost everything
Trying
Trying to do everything right
Right time
Right mood
Right colour
Right smile

Right you
Wrong me
Right wrong
Wrong right
I tried
Tried too hard
Cried
Cried too hard….
You wept my tears
And said
"don't you cry like this…
don't show your emotions to the world
you forgot you were my entire universe
entire cosmos
I showed my lament only to you
But slowly you got sicken
Its time I felt
You should be left alone
But I will love you crazily from far
My right to love you
Your right to disregard…."

GOSSIPS

POEM NO. 9

Beloved...

What do I say! oh! My beloved
My beloved is like a moonlight
Lighting my dark alleys
Where I used to walk alone…
My beloved is like those rain drops
Giving life to my lifeless soul
He is the depth of seas
So deep where I bury my sorrows
He is like those white pearls
Adorns me like no one ever has
Like those tiny silk worms…
Creating art and cover my naked heart…
You know my beloved
He is like those great mountains
Protecting me from all things harsh
Like that soft breeze
Caressing my body all the time
He is my shelter, my anchor
He is my kite, my string
He is soft like snow

And valiant like the storms
He changes his colour
The colour that I want to drown myself in
Such care, such tender heart
Such altruistic attachment
I meditate on
My beloved….

HARMONY IN LOVE

POEM NO. 10

Gone So Far...

You've gone so far, so far
That I can't even ask you
"how are you?
Are you doing all fine ?
Are you spending nights
Gazing at the stars
Are you walking those
Streets now… alone"
Are you still talking
Like you used to
Are you still carefree
And child like
Do you still cry
While watching Notting Hill
And keep humming
My favourite songs…
Your dimples which peek
When you smile
Do you still remember me?
Sometimes, very less

May be only for a second
Do you?
Do you still visit your old house?
Where you were raised
The place we wanted to visit together
But….
You left before we could
You left before I could experience
Your love
Do you hold someone else's hands now
The way you promised
You would mine…
Do you?
Do you?
Do you?

IT'S SHOWTIME

POEM NO. 11

The Wall...

Under the clear blue sky
There is an empty wall
A wall so big
But still so aimless
Vacant, worthless, useless
Sputter all over
Impress every where
Just like you may say
Humans used it
In an abusive colour
But the wall stood strong
Loving the locals
Loving those song birds
Those tiny pure hearts
Who often took shelter
In the depressions
And brought joy
Like the empty hearts
Who walk pass the wall
And look at it with lust and love

Touching it everywhere
But the wall so steady
So strong
Who built it?
Creator of All
Existence who else
Life and His Wall…

KISS ME DEEP

POEM NO. 12

The Corner Café...

I will meet you
At the Corner Café
Sharp at five
Wearing my grey shirt
As grey as can be…
Just like me
As I lack emotions now
As I lack sentiments
As I lack so so many things
You reminded me every day
So less I was for you
Mere nothing
Only a human with immense love
For my one and only
Not enough to be loved back
Right?
Not good enough to meet your
High class friends
Not sufficient to wipe your tears
You were always looking for something more

Which I wasn't for sure
I was simple shabby a vase with cracks all over
Who was ready every day to take up challenges
For you…
Couldn't fit in your high heels
And trendy tweet ups
Not a reel person
Just a tea lover
Enjoying the rains
And long, long walks
Touching your soft hands
And gazing at your sparkly eyes
Why suddenly the text then
Why this pain in the voice calls I hear…?
I will come for sure
Sharp at five
At the Corner Café
For you dear….

LADY LOVE

POEM NO. 13

Punish Me...

Punish me
Punish me for loving you
Punish me for loving you secretly
Punish me for loving you in my prayers
Punish me for bunking school
And standing in front of yours…
Punish me for saving my coins
And buying you those sour lollies…
Punish me for stealing those Laddoos
From papa's shop
Because you loved them
Punish me for getting admission
In your college
And leaving my scope of
Going world wide…
Punish me to feel the way
You never felt for me
Punish me your way
And make me a hero
A love lost war

Losing to you
Is winning to myself
Punish me
For the stupid heart I have
Which you never took
But which I gave only to you
Punish me
For all that makes me
A crazy secret lover
Of you!!!

LAST NIGHT

CARE HELP LOVE
SUPPORT
KIND SMI
RESPECT
KIND RESPECT ATTRACTION
SUPPORT LOVE HELP SUPPORT COMPASS
TRUST TRUTH SMILE CARE
CARE SMILE
LOVE HONESTY
SMILE CARE
RESPECT KIN
LOVE
TRUTH
HONESTY
KIND CAR
SMILE
LOVE
RESPECT RESPECT
LOVE
CARE
SMILE
LOVE
TRUST
KIND
LOVE TRUTH
LOYALTY
TRUTH
SMILE
COMPASSION
LOVE
CARE
TRUST
KIN

POEM NO. 14

Pleasing Till My Last...

I tried to please your soul…
In so many ways
Concealing my dark circles
With high end make up…
Wearing the long dress
You wanted me to
Stood in front of your mates
Praising how good a partner
You are so caring…
While your eyes gazing
At other lassies…
Their smooth skin
Deep cleft
Lustful eyes
Black hair
Remember once I wanted to wear
A red dress
The little red dress
Your disapproval
Came as a blow

On my youthful face
I smiled and approved
Why?
Why did I?
I should have gusted
At you
I should have
Stood for myself
But the pain
I was in love
With you
And the pain
And now here I am
Standing a lone
In our party
Like a stranger among all
Your gazing eyes
Never stopped at me though….

LIPS DON'T LIE

POEM NO. 15

At Your Convenience...

When nothing comes out
Of anything
Then I am your friend
After giving away
My heart
My beloved tells me
You are just a friend
Friendship you say
And rip me apart
And forget the love you promised
The promise I was feeding on
All the days and months and years
After loving me
Like a man loves his woman
You say I am a friend
After assuring a life together
You say I am a friend
Is this a beloved
Who turns into a friend?
Or always a friend

Whom you mistook
As a beloved for a moment!
Alas! Everything comes out of nothing
Every beloved turns to be a friend
When nothing comes out of nothing
As there wasn't anything
From the very beginning....

LOYAL AS A DOG

POEM NO. 16

The Day That Turned Into Night

Yesterday, the day that became a night
The hours of darkness that I spend
Smiling, silently whimpering
Was remarkably memorable
My beloved showered me…
With words…
Words that inspired me
To live differently
To think wisely
To smile without a reason
My beloved said
It was me who inspired him
To move away from all things attractive
It was me who founded his faults
And made him what he is
It was me who dominated him
And made him a warrior
My beloved hated me
And my past
And my high heels, my lipstick mark

My red dress, unfit for his grey shirt
My blingy heart, not a match
For his simple soul
And yet six years passed….
Six years, sixth spring time
All so sham, a hoax
He said vividly I remember
He said you're not mine anymore
My beloved reminded me
The sacrifices he did
True were his offerings
True his love
I thus couldn't count mine
Alas I said smiling
Holding on to his strong hands
You are free, from a queen like me
Explore and find true love
High heels, lipstick marks
Are too tough to handle…
My love!!!

ME AND MYSELF

POEM NO. 17

The Red Dot

A red vermilion dot
A big one
Coming forward, pushing away the crowd
Hair rolled up into a bun
Black kohl almond eyes
Lips moistened with balm
Cotton saree draped
A little wet with sweat
I was sitting on the foot path
Begging…
Begging for money…
No, no, no I want
But was begging for something
Something such invaluable
Sources…
I was begging for time…
I was begging for attention…
Yesss, begging for companionship
My Merc, parked across the street
I was begging for someone

The vermilion dot came
Close to me....
Sat down and hugged me tight
She looked so familiar
Someone I know
Yet I couldn't recall
Couldn't smile
Couldn't cry
Couldn't hug her tight
She whispered
Its you… its you
Get up, dance, feel free…
You have you…
You have me…
Love yourself
Get wet in the rains
Cry and shout
Let go of what you think is pain
Magic is inside
Open the doors
Let the light come out
Unlearn what's right
Wrong is just a word
You were always right your way
Love me love you
You and me are same
You and me are same....

MUSCLE MANIAC

POEM NO. 18

Shameful Glory...

He touched me…
My lady parts were being felt
Ten years of summers
Had just passed
And he never cared
Just played
I cried….
Came running to my dad
He laughed, Maa was sad
That was years ago…
Now just a story
Even when it was a truth
It was shameful
It was a lie
A story
A shameful glory
The trauma it caused
Remains safely inside my core
And follows me
Like a traveler

Following the shore
The memories like the waves
Touching the traveler's feet
Ah! The lady I am now
The slate inside me not so neat
The smell of alcohol
Such a disgusting odor
Screams out bothers me
Such a dark room
Such a dark heart
I fear black now
I sleep in the light
As I want everything right
Not for me but for the soul
For the spirit which wants to live
For the life which my Maa gave
For the life I produced
I want to live
I want to live…

MUSIC HEALS US ALL

POEM NO. 19

Till Death Do Us Apart...

When my Beloved
Adorns herself beautifully
With jewels I presented her
Every summer
And walks the streets
The city of joy
The beats of life
Come to a pause
The walking by
Smiles and shies…
The young girl
Stares and in awe
The butterflies' follows
Whispering amongst them
Such beauty never saw…
One summer I gave her a song
She draped it around her neck
Like a scarf of passion
The next summer I offered her
The music

She wore it as a waist string
Around her slender yet plump
Waist…
Another summer she asked me
For my time
I gave her that too
And now as she walks
I walk beside…
And see my lady
Looking bewitching
Enchanting like a potion
Of mystical hue
Sparkling in her own way
While the city looks dull
Making me a proud lover
Of her soul
Not controlling her whimsical
Loving and carefree aura
As I take pride in letting her
Lead…
And steal the show and the hearts
Whose heart I owe
My beloved, and I am hers
The world can see
Till death do us part…

NATURE'S TALK

POEM NO. 20

The Neverending Search...

Lying on the bed
I cried I cried
Age is just a number you said
Lying as a patient
I cried and cried
It's the pain
I want to get rid off
It's the time
That's not ending no more
I waited
And still am
My eyes still staring at the door
Wishing to see you one last time
Before I leave
Before I forget
How you look!
Come, connect, care
One day, I asked
A day
Twenty-four hours

Was all I asked from your
Entire life
I wanted to love you
And still, as I write my
Last chapter
You haven't yet
Gifted me
With your hours
Time is running
Like the wild horse
And you still so disinclined
Is it so difficult
To just pretend
For a moment
When you loved me
For that one day
Burying my fuselage
In your warmth
I forgot it was just
An appetite
Still I want to believe
It was love
And nothing less or more
I want to rest now
And die in your crest…

PEACEFUL AFFAIR

POEM NO. 21

My Clingy Beloved...

My beloved left me
He said I was being too clingy
Too much expectations
Made him feel so claustrophobic
That one fine day
He said his feelings were gone
I smiled and said
Giving up is not that I believe in
I will try
Remind you of those beautiful walks
We shared
Behind the church gate
Those long nights when
We spoke
Like the night was an endless sea
We were swimming in
Those long glances across the class rooms
When we spoke more
Those long fights
Which ended with kisses and hugs

All this
And he laughed
Was I funny
Or were those moments just so trivial
For him now
Your tantrums my love
Egomaniacal is the word
He used to describe me
Inward looking
Self-absorbed
Opportunistic
Thoughtless
Self-pleasing
He just kept on and on
Bombarding me with words
That meant only one thing
He was never really in
Love with me
He was in love with a
Presence
With an availability
With an appearance….
He was searching for something more
Spacious
Something more liberating
And my love was so overwhelming
So immature

Hopeless and dreadful…
So what I did was
I left his hands
And set him free
Free to explore
And find the sky he searched for
My love was no sky
It was a white cloud in the sky
Small and comforting
Soft and warm
Tiny and ours
Clingy but just his…
And he was looking
For not the cloud
But the sky…

RED TEAR DROPS

POEM NO. 22

Soulmates...

That starry night
You were in your
Black Armani
And I was wearing a
Red saree
In your luxurious car
You drove me out
Our first date
Official…
I thought we will be driving
Driving to a seven star studded
Opulent eatery…
But…
The car took us to
The highway
And slowed down
At a distance
You took my hands
And we entered
Entered a small Dhaba

I was so at bay
Looking around
All humongous men
Nine or ten
Looked at us peeped from
Corners
And here we were
Two crazy nuts
Crazy in love
Crazy with the man
Sitting across my sight
You were different
Not one of those
Who pretend
Who make lotuses
Look like lilies
Who forget their roots
So, you in your Armani
Held my strong spirit
And said
I started here
This is who I am
Once a looser
And always want to lose
To you
Eating at simple joints
But with you

Trickling from those corners
Expensive fabrics wet
And the red girl
Proposed
To the dark man
Couldn't let go
Of this heart
For whom priorities meant
Roots
Creating magic through moments
Was more important
Than brands
And our first date became
A beautiful story of life...

RELUCTANT LOVE

POEM NO. 23

Just That Once...

I looked at her once
Just that once
Became a stare forever
I just looked at her once
Just that once
Became a lifelong legacy
I just looked at her once
Just that once
Became the reason to live
I just looked at her once
Just that once
Made me fear death…
Her glance…
That happened to stop
At me
By chance…

REST IN PEACE

POEM NO. 24

Memories Of You...

My scars
You said they are beautiful
You said
My scars
Remind you that
I am strong
I am tough
And then you said
You will never leave my side
You promised
We will build
Our abode
With great warmth
With passion of gratitude
The day will come
When we will share
Each other's name
Each other's cup
You promised
We will have kids together

And give them the love
We never got
And then I saw
Among those white cotton like floaties
Your cold soul
I called your names millions of time
And you never answered me
All your dreams
Which I need to attain
Are floating
In the air
Your smell
Your voice calling me…
You punished me
Punished your only own self
Leaving me alone forever
Ripped me into pieces
But your memories
Still give the solidity to me
I will life with the glories
I found with you
Here in our world
Of our love
As u seek me
From above…

SELF JUDGEMENTAL

POEM NO. 25

My Master...

Your shadow
Kept following me
Till I reached home
I know it follows me
All the time
I am not alone
When it's raining
I am not alone
When there is a curfew
Your shadow
Is surrounding me
All the time
"Shadow go and tell him
To come and meet me bodily"
"He can't
His body lies in the grave
Master told me to be with you
Hence left me behind…"

SELF LOVE

POEM NO. 26

Lovingly My Own...

In the night
I stay awake
Most of the time
Trying to find me
In the darkness
Where I can see myself better
My mum thought I am mad
My dad said she is sad
I ran to my room
And started laughing
They never knew the truth
I was a girl
With a heart of a lad
I suffered from pain
I was hurt
I was used again and again
My emotions thrown away
Played with
Juggling in between times
When all I was gifted

With was blames and names…
This so called cultivated circles
Circled me with hatred
And unearthly behaviour
I tried to be a part of
Womanhood
Fall in love with men
But I found myself
In love with me more
Than ever…
Loving yourself first
Is what my gender taught me
I walk the pride walk
Everyday
Every single day
Belongs to me
The way I look at myself
Is how the world should see

SELF OBSESSED

POEM NO. 27

My Fake Existence...

A fake consolation
A fake smile
A fake I love you
A fake your mine
A fake situation ship
A fake fall… to win hearts
A fake life to balance the birth
A fake lover to blind souls
A fake Instagram to stop trolls
A fake way to impress all
A fake brand to show the world
A fake group a Wanna be type
A fake ambition I want to climb high
A fake argument I win I win
A fake loss a relief within
A fake love a burden to handle
A fake let go to console my tears
A fake you is all I deserved
A fake me is all you searched for
A fake life let make it real
A fake real let's make it worthwhile

SITUATION SHIP

POEM NO. 28

That Day That Never Happened...

Remember that day
When we fought
Like we never fought before
Remember that day
When you turned away
And never looked back
Remember that day
When your phone didn't stop ringing
Remember that day
When my calls were all unanswered
Remember that day
When my birth became a curse
Remember that day
When you said your life was a pain
All for me
Remember that day
When I kept folding my hands
Without reason
Remember that day
When I realized it was me

Who became the culprit
The sinner
The evil spirit
Yes I remember that day
While you forgot so easily....
And behaved so casually
As if nothing ever happened
Qualities I learned
My love
That changed me
Into a dead soul....

SOLITUDE

POEM NO. 29

Kiss Of Misery...

I asked you for a kiss
A kiss that I will remember
A kiss that I will honor
A kiss that I will miss
A life and more
And you showered me with
Care, kindness, time
I can't handle so much
Altogether
A kiss was all I desired
But you made me yours forever
What intentions were
Roaming in your heart
You must have been in love
With me
For a moment at least
As time was the most precious
Anklet you made me wear
But all I desired was a
Kiss of detachment

The hardest tale
Then came after
You left! Me with memories
And said they were gestures
Of my friendship
And nothing more
I have mastered the trick
The trick to live a content life
You said.
And leave you miserable
For the rest of yours!

SPIRITUAL SIN

POEM NO. 30

Saving You From Me...

My beloved for you
I wanted to change every bit of me
I never wanted you to love me back
But, yes I wanted to be around you
To smell your fragrance of jasmine
That's all
Like Rumi said
I wanted to love you in silence
But my eyes spoke loudly
Which you failed to hear
My beloved I wanted to know
To read
Every fragment of your feeling
Wanted to save you from the pain
I saw you went through everyday
But my helplessness
My narcissistic behavior
Knew I couldn't make you smile
If I come close you will only burn
Such is love such is devotion

Knowing I am hurtful, I am staying miles apart
From the only one I love
And will love forever
Knowing I am selfish, I am trying to change
But I see
Your pain is growing
And like a helpless soul
I am viewing and staying hushed
Don't misunderstand me
My love
I am fain hearted
Can't take a step forward towards you
Forgive me
For letting you down always
When I can see in your eyes
Searching for my yes
My hands
My warmth
I can't give you none
I can't....

STEAMY STORM

POEM NO. 31

Reliving One Sided Love...

While I was walking
Those roads we once
Walked together
Memories were waving by
Some smiled, some tear eyed
But all were very dear to my heart
To my fervor
Those roads had witnessed
Our newly found love
Those nooks and corners knew
How sweetly you kissed me
Every little chance you got
That lamp-post knew
What time we would reach there
Together
How invaluable!
That when now you no longer wish to be here
I come and smile and feel us
Those stair cases we walked up
Remember! How close you held me

Closest to your heart beat
Eyes looked away
And the charm kept lingering on
Even today I feel it
I sense it
In that empty stair case
Where you left me alone
We still stand…
Remember those Tibetan joints
Where we went for some
Hot wontons
Raining outside
New fondness shilly shallying
Deep inside!
Now you must be sitting there
Holding your new loves
Soft delicate palm
More precious than us
More matured as they say
But memories that belong to me
Will be mine till the last
The ATM booth
The fight right across the street
How the stars gazed at us
How you threw your bag
And I kept weeping
Then again our hands tied

Love was there
Those childish arguments were love
Which felt heavy on you
You left out of fear
But those roads, that joint
Forever and ever
Mine
Only mine!

SEW IT ALL UP

POEM NO. 32

Just Like That...

Hi! Want to be friends with you
Just like that
You know I lost something
Just like that
Your number
Just like that
You are so different
A someone I have never met before
Just like that
Can I look into you're
Deep eyes! Just like that
Your messed up life
Your messy hair
Don't worry
Life was unfair
I will make it up
For you
Just like that
You want to settle
I can help

Just like that
You have done sin
I still adore you
You have loved many
Still I love you
Just like that
I will ghost you
Then come back
Then assure you
How busy I have been
All these days
Just like that
By now
I know you love me
I have fed you with
Dreams you always wanted
To live for
Like a toy how beautifully
I could play with you
Just like that
Made love to you
Without you even
Realizing that
I just wanted to make you
Feel even worse
Just like that
We are just friends

Please grow up
And do take care
Just like that!!!

THE BANJARA GIRL

POEM NO. 33

Prayers Of Love...

When I pray folding my hands
My parted lips take your name
When I pray bowing my head
I bow my head down to you
When I pray with tears in my eyes
My tears want to wash away your pain
When I pray with immense pain in my heart
It's your success that brings me joy
When I pray with doubt in my mind
It's my worries for you my love
When I pray selflessly
It's your selfless love you gave me
When I pray with love only for Him
Its only Him I pray for…

THE CAGED SOUL

POEM NO. 34

In Silence...

I know, I know, I know
You see me everyday
You hide yourself somewhere
Somewhere in the crowd
While you're walking past
The hours
You see me
You make sure your own way
Whether I am fine
Whether I smile
Whether I am eating
Whether my days are turning into
Hours of darkness
With joy and not sorrow
I know
Your birds are flying around me
Taking care of my path
So I don't get lost
In my thoughts
Thoughts of losing you

Thoughts of loving you
You see me and the drops
That fall in the night
But restrict yourself
From wiping them
As you know
You won't be there
To wipe them always
Is this what love is?
What magic of
Love is!
Loving someone
And not letting them
Know!!
Then I am sure
When one knows
It's all heart break
It's all over
Life is magical
When you love
In secret
In disguise
In distance
In silence
In camouflage
In blur....

THE CAT MAN

POEM NO. 35

The Toxic Ship...

It was a toxic ship
Toxic as can be
Toxic like when you breath
You feel like choking
Toxic like when you eat nothing
And you still feel full
Toxic like when you bath
You feel like standing in their numb
A minute or two more and more
Toxic like when they shout
You feel like hiding forever
Toxic like when they come home
You feel like never opening the door
Toxic like when you think
You feel nothing yet helpless
Toxic like when you decide
You have the power
To break through
And you do that!!!

THE CRAZY CRY

POEM NO. 36

The Deep Blue Ocean...

The ocean invited me
The vastness of my friend
Was so scary to me
At first I was so hesitant
Hesitant to close to Him
But the deep blue foams
But the thin horizon
But the lovely sight
Was so calm, that
I was only drawn
Drawn to Him
He whispered
In my ears
Look at me
We are similar
How? I wondered
The vastness you see
I see in you
That's why we both are so alone
We give, we are the givers

We listen
We feel
We talk but to ourselves
We are misunderstood
Yet we are the true protectors
We love
Even when unloved
We return
All that does not belong to us
Tears come out
Which are never seen
Which was never felt
My friend
We are similar
So, come and stand in front of me
When you feel lonely
We both are similar…
So when you feel
I feel the same…

THE EYECONIC VIEW

POEM NO. 37

My Magnanimous Self...

My self-love is so magnanimous
My self-love is so pious
My self-love is so righteous
That I left all those
Who wanted to destroy me
My self-love was an out come
Was an answer
To all of them who mistreated
Who dared to brake me!
With their over sweet gestures
With their over fake oaths
They wanted
Me to believe
They loved me they said
More than I could love
Myself!
Proving them all wrong
I could rise as a phoenix
They failed in their efforts
They failed in their loyalty

They failed in their romance
They failed in their safety
They failed in equality
They failed in their intentions
But I rose in loving me
Shamed them
Showed them
What love is
What self-love actually meant
How to love they all bluffed
While I could only adore!

THE PAINFUL EXISTENCE

POEM NO. 38

The Other Woman...

Can't be a home breaker
Can't be a heart wrecker
When life throws stone
Can't be a stone picker
Love born
Out of senses
Love that was not in reels
But was real
Don't name her as a gold digger
Lies used for nourishing
Her broken soul
A mere toy
To play with
Don't blame
For her being coy
Her candour nature
With your falsehood
Your manhood
Your vulnerability
Used as a trick
With brilliance

Then don't call her a
Spouse snatcher
Playing a victim
Playing a feeble heart
Was never her role play
Was never her card
One chance
And she will show the universe
His ways
Why the pink hearts
Always shamed
And why
The blue bloods
Never
When their lips met
Never for a moment
He felt....
For the lives
He left
His hypocrisy
His drama
Always went unnoticed
Notice was only sent to her
Defamed shamed
Gifted to her
She is no home breaker
She is not a heart wrecker!!!

THE PORTRAIT

POEM NO. 39

Ment To Be Mental...

My beloved was strange
We met under the sun
One fine day
His eyes were deep
His smile so bright
I couldn't resist
And drowned in his arms
He lifted me and made me sit
On a bed of petals
And spoke words
As sweet as nectar
Made me feel
The most special bae
His smell so different
Like the fresh rain waters
Like the first moist mud
Of the season
Like the smell you always
Want to keep with you
His arms so warm

I was painted in his colour
His colour of love
Black
I started enacting him
I chanted words
He taught me
That's how powerful
His magic was on me
And then came that
Night
When he abruptly
Took a pause
From loving me
A pause so horrific
So long
His deep eyes
Became a pit
His smile so cunning
The bed of roses
Were thorns of poison
And no words
Not a single sound
From his mouth
His smell choking me to death
A trap
A map
A gap

It was just a bling, a show
Of his charm
There was nothing true
To the story
Just a de ja vu
I saw since I was young
It was all inside
No one to blame
For this mental game!!!

THE PURE ENCLOSURE

POEM NO. 40

Strangers And Their Love...

Don't talk to strangers
You may end up in loving them
Don't walk with strangers
You may end up walking their path
Don't laugh with strangers
You may end up crying for them
Don't cry with strangers
You may end up being their night pillow
Don't look into their eyes
You may never want to look at any after them
Don't talk to strangers
You may end up falling in love with them
Don't share your deep hidden life with them
They might become your confidante
Whom you may just loose after a mile
After a while
So when you bump into
A stranger
Just move away
When strangers pass by

Just turn around
When they want say
A hi!

THE PURE HEARTS

POEM NO. 41

Being Yourself...

We are all lonely
At the end of it all
We are left alone
When all is gone
Like the empty wall
We are left alone
So why don't we
Look at ourselves
With a little more love
With a little more care
Why self-love
Is often misunderstood
As selfishness
Why looking after, ourselves
Can't be a positive anecdote
To the poison
That society wants to
Inject us with
Why can't we just be
Just be ourselves
Why loneliness

Will bring tears
And not satisfaction
To our soul
Why being alone
Is often looked as
Someone isolated
Why being alone
Is not a bliss
Yes, it is
Only when we can love
Us!
Appreciate our flaws
With a kiss!
Why judging eyes
Will decide
Who we are
Why loving someone
Will make us look
Like villains
When all we were was tricked
To fall
And now when we self-love
We annoy all!
This hypocrisy
This pretend concern
Through it away
Now that it's your turn….

THE REBEL

POEM NO. 42

Un Prescribed Meds...

The meds you prescribed
Didn't work for me
The un prescribed meds
I took worked wonders
Expensive jewels
Branded clothes
Lavish hotels
Luxe life
Royal carriages
Didn't work for me
Long self walks
Long self-talks
Worked wonders...

THE TRAVELLER

POEM NO. 43

Kintsugi...

You are so beautiful
You are so perfect
He said
And then she showed him
Her scars
Ugly as hell
Raw as raw
And deep as the Pacific
You are even more beautiful
Than I thought
You are so real
So pure
So simple
Such true a soul
Who showed her scars
With-out any hesitant act
Let me love your scars first
And then the rest….
The scars that define you
The scars that made you

Who you are
I love who you are
And the past you carry
Your scars I will treasure
And make you mine
And your present precious
Like you are
Broken
But a star!!
The Japanese work of art
That breaks
But heals with gold
And becomes invaluable
The unbreakable!!!!

TIME AND TALES

POEM NO. 44

Whom To Choose...

The mountain
The ocean
The tree
All welcomed me
When you turned away
Mountain said
Love me lover
I am strong
Will protect you
Like no other
Will calm you
When you need
Come to me
Forever!!
Ocean said
After the night passes
Come to me
I will clean you
Bathe you
Make you fresh

As a flower
You are to me
Be your best friend
And listen to you
My waters
Will keep your secret safe
Tree said
I will wait
Forever for you
Come to me
When you are left with nothing
When you have no shelter or food
I will provide you with that
And more…

TO MY DEAREST SELF

POEM NO. 45

Distant Love...

He said
I have loved many skins
She said
Are you in love with mine too
He said
It's your soul
I am in love with
Because your soul gives me
The ultimate pleasure
I found in none
She said
Love me from a distance then…

TRANS-FIGURES CHARM

POEM NO. 46

Dreams And More...

I have salt on my body
I have you in my mind
I have memories
That I cherish
When you are nearby.

I have love in my heart
That I give you all the time

I have prayers in my words
Which I read all the time
I have coins in my pocket
Which I save for our future

I have dreams in my eyes
Which I see with you
I have yearnings
Which are special
And I want them to come true...

TRIBAL LOVE

POEM NO. 47

Coward Lover...

kiss me tonight
but not tomorrow
as today I am still yours
tomorrow his forever...

when the time was right
you looked away the other side
and today in the last hour
you say love is our...

how can I stop this now
how can I end it all
the black potion
does the magic
time so small...

let's drink it together
you and me
and be together
amidst mountains and the sea...

you ran away hearing this
so, I drank the potion
what a bliss
you coward
you fraud
you came for lust
not love
my love
but I will haunt you now
to make things tough...

TRIBAL TALE

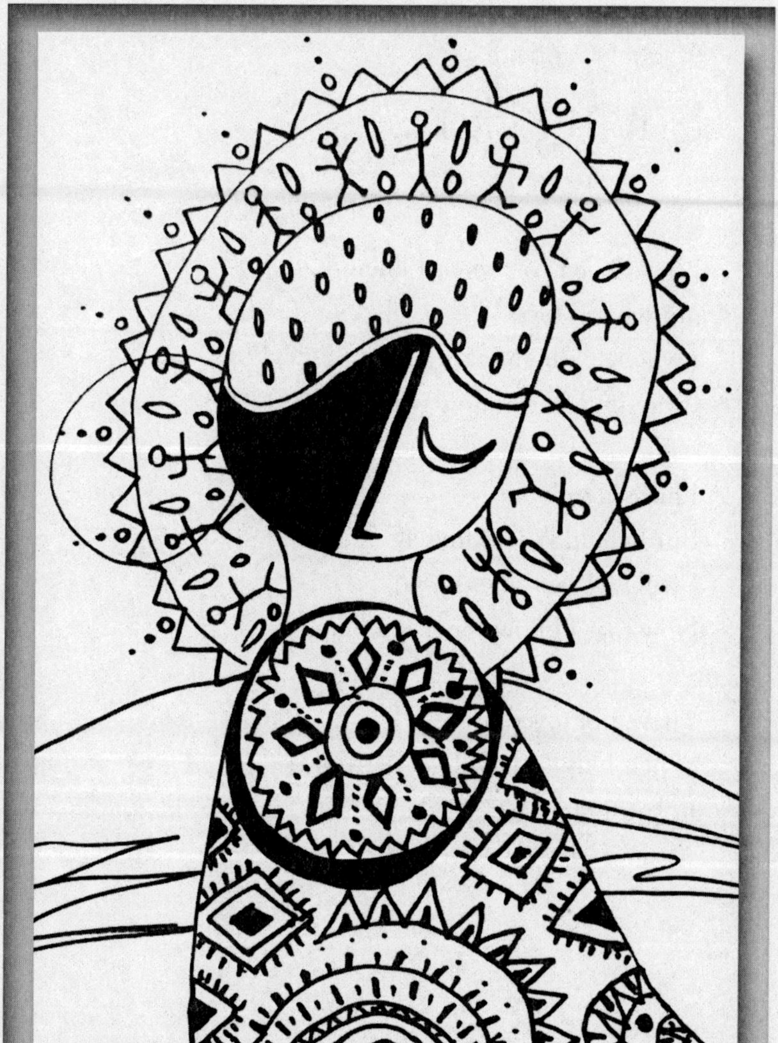

POEM NO. 48

Saving Her...

I have loved you when I knew
not what is love
I will be with you
Even now that I know what is love.

I have saved you
But I couldn't save myself
I will save her
Now that I know she needs help.

I have destroyed us
When I saw you will get destroyed
I can't destroy her
As she is already destroyed.

UNIQUE IN OUR OWN WAYS

POEM NO. 49

Lost Love...

A boy was playing in the garden
Every day he came to play
One day he saw a flower
He liked the flower so much
That he shed his tears to wet
the soil bed under her.

The flower blossomed as never before
And then one day he stopped coming
But the flower kept on blooming
As she knew the bigger she grew
The boy could see her even from a distant land
And thus, their story ended
Unheard of
But the garden witnessed it
And so, the story lingered in every corner of it...

WEDDING BLUES

POEM NO. 50

Haunting Tunes...

My lips were hurting
When I tried to take your name

My heart was aching
when I tried to take away my pain

My ribs had swollen
When I pulled your breath from me

My legs bruised all over
When I walked till your doorstep to see

To see that you were not with me
"Open the door" I shouted for hours

Neighbours looked as if I was mad
They couldn't see the me so sad

The door remained closed
As it should be

Go back where you came from
The door is not for thee

Alas I walked back with my bruised legs
Swollen ribs
Aching heart
Hurting lips
To where I belong

Thus, I led my life
Peace was long gone

Then I died
But my ghost still walks

To that doorstep
Like a vagabond
To seek solace...

ACKNOWLEDGEMENTS

TO MY BEAUTIFUL CHILDREN, EKALAVYA & EKANTIKA

My heartfelt gratitude goes out to all the unsung poets, whose verses have profoundly enriched every language in this world.

A big thank you to everyone who has helped me grow, especially my family, who have been my constant support system. Your presence and inspiration make me whole.

Special thanks to the team at *The Book Bakers*, one of the leading literary agencies in the country, for believing in my work, shaping my literary journey, and encouraging me to experiment with different poetic styles. My literary agent, Suhail Mathur, has consistently shown faith in my writing, particularly with this book of poems. I feel lucky to be associated with him and his team.

I extend my sincere thanks to my dynamic publisher, Anecdote Publishing, for their belief and faith in this book.

In Between The Lines is a book of poems for readers of all genders and ages, to delve into the treasures of emotions hidden within the human heart. I sincerely hope that everyone enjoys my poems and my book and my sketches as much as I have enjoyed creating them.